Cold Storage

A NEW PLAY IN TWO ACTS

By Ronald Ribman

D0999472

SAMUEL FRENCH, INC.

25 West 45th Street   NEW YORK 10036
7623 Sunset Boulevard   HOLLYWOOD 90046
LONDON   *TORONTO*

LYCEUM THEATRE

A Shubert Organization Theatre

Gerald Schoenfeld, *Chairman*   Bernard B. Jacobs, *President*

Produced on Broadway in 1977 by Clare Nichtern and Ashton Springer in Association With Irene Miller

present

MARTIN BALSAM   LEN CARIOU

in

COLD STORAGE

a new play by
RONALD RIBMAN
with
RUTH RIVERA

Set, Costume and
Scenic Design by
KARL EIGSTI

Lighting Design by
WILLIAM MINTZER

Directed by

FRANK CORSARO

"Cold Storage" was presented at the American Place Theatre
in New York City April 1977.

The Producers and Theatre Management are Members
of The League of New York Theatres and Producers, Inc.

ACT ONE

A hospital roof garden in New York City

ACT TWO

The roof garden, early evening the same day

CAST
(In order of appearance)

RICHARD LANDAU

MISS MADURGA

JOSEPH PARMIGIAN

Cold Storage

ACT ONE

SCENE: *A hospital roof garden in New York City. A number of tables and chairs are placed about the roof, along with a scattering of artificial bushes and plants. In the appointments of the roof garden and in the architecture of the building itself, there is a quiet beaux arts elegance.*

ON RISE: *This June day is pleasant.* RICHARD LANDAU, *a man in his mid-forties, dressed in pajamas and a rather handsome looking robe, sits Downstage in a wheelchair. His eyes are shut, and in his hand he holds a candy bar. As he sits there, motionless for the moment, it is difficult to tell if he is asleep or simply lost in his own thoughts. Several yards behind him a nurse,* MISS MADURGA, *sits by herself, reading an issue of Vogue Magazine.* MISS MADURGA *is young, slender, and attractive—a woman who obviously takes care of her physical appearance. For some moments there is silence on the roof, a silence broken only by the occasional turning of a magazine page, and then* JOSEPH PARMIGIAN, *a man totally confined to his wheelchair, wheels himself onto the roof garden and into this almost motionless tableau.* PARMIGIAN *is a man in his mid-sixties. Over his robe and pajamas he has spread a small blanket on his lap. The nurse, busy with her magazine, scarcely*

5

seems to notice his arrival. PARMIGIAN *glances at her for a second as she turns a page and then moves Downstage, coming to a stop near* LANDAU. *When he sees that* LANDAU'S *eyes are closed and there is no possibility for conversation, he leaves out a little cry of disgust, and turns away. For some seconds silence returns again, and then* LANDAU *begins making small sounds of agitation, his face contorting into an angry grimace. As* PARMIGIAN *stares at him,* LANDAU *raises the candy bar in his hand, and begins to crush it under great tension.*

PARMIGIAN. You're squashing it. (LANDAU *doesn't seem to hear.*) You're squashing it!

LANDAU. (*His eyes blinking open.*) What?

PARMIGIAN. If you don't want it, give it to me. (LANDAU *looks down at the candy bar, realizing perhaps for the first time what he has done.*) There's no point in squashing something just because you don't want it. (PARMIGIAN *wheels himself over to* LANDAU *and, taking the candy bar out of his hands, begins unwrapping it.*) That fat Puerto Rican your private duty nurse?

LANDAU. What fat Puerto Rican?

PARMIGIAN. (*Without turning his head, angrily gesturing over his shoulder with his thumb at* MISS MADURGA.) That! That! What other fat Puerto Rican is there out here?

LANDAU. Yes, she's my private duty nurse, but I hardly think she's fat.

PARMIGIAN. Is that so? Is that your evaluation, Mr. Whatever-your-name-is?

LANDAU. Richard Landau.

PARMIGIAN. Well, let me tell you something, Mr. Richard Landau. They're all fat, and the longer you stay here the fatter they get. (*Takes a bite out of the candy bar, makes a sour face, and tosses it back into* LANDAU's *lap.*) Keep your candy. It's stale. (*Crosses Left to Downstage Center.*)

LANDAU. Miss Madurga is from Honduras, not Puerto Rico.

PARMIGIAN. Is that what she told you? Honduras, huh? Honduras?

LANDAU. Yes.

PARMIGIAN. And you believed that?

LANDAU. Yes, I believed that. Why shouldn't I?

PARMIGIAN. Because she's a liar. She used to be my private duty nurse before I was forced to let her go because of her overweight problem, and she told me she was from Guatemala. Guatemala! (MADURGA *looks up. Turning his head and shouting back at* MISS MADURGA.) Fat chance Guatemala! (*The* NURSE *momentarily lowers her magazine, exchanges a glance with* PARMIGIAN, *and then returns to her reading.*) They're never from Puerto Rico, you see. They're always from Honduras, or Guatemala, or Panama, or Equador, or Tierra del Fuego. No matter where they tell you they're from, it's never Puerto Rico. They just don't want to admit it.

LANDAU. Why wouldn't they want to admit it?

PARMIGIAN. Because it's not classy enough for them . . . because they're so used to giving us cock and bull stories they don't know what the truth is anymore—how do I know? I caught one of them walking around in a sari with a spot between her eyes and a diamond sticking out of her nose. She was telling all the patients she was from Ceylon, or Borneo, or someplace. She even had a bagful of tea leaves to prove it. The only flaw in her disguise was that every time she wheeled me in for my cobalt treatment I could see a half-finished banana sticking out of her cleavage. You ever see anyone from Ceylon walking around with a half-finished banana sticking out of her cleavage?

LANDAU. I really don't know what they walk around with in Ceylon. I've never been there.

PARMIGIAN. Well, neither have I. Who the hell's ever been to Ceylon? But I can tell you one thing: their national fruit sure ain't no banana! You want some advice, Landau? No matter how weak you get, don't let them know it. You can't throw the covers off the bed, tell them you feel as strong as a bull elephant. The first sign of weakness they see in you, the truth goes out the window. You'll never hear it again. A five hundred ton meteorite hits you in the head, they'll tell you a chip of paint fell off the goddamn ceiling. Bastards! (MISS MADURGA *puts her magazine down and stands up. Although she moves silently, and* PARMIGIAN *appears not to be looking in her direction, she's hardly gotten to her feet before he's aware of it. He speaks without turning his head to face her.*) Going in for a little smoke, Miss Madurga? You don't have to hide in the broom closet with the rest of them. We know all the doctors and nurses are smoking in the broom closet.

MISS MADURGA. (*Walking over to them.*) I'm just going in to get something to eat, Mr. Parmigian. I haven't had my lunch yet. (*Crosses Right above* PARMIGIAN *to* LANDAU. *Turning to her patient.*) Can I get you anything before I go, Mr. Landau?

LANDAU. No, I'm fine, thank you.

PARMIGIAN. You can get me something.

MISS MADUGRA. What would you like, Mr. Parmigian?

PARMIGIAN. Sixty thousand dollars so I can pay my hospital bill for the week.

MISS MADURGA. Just try to rest, Mr. Parmigian. It doesn't help getting yourself excited all the time.

PARMIGIAN. You call this excitement, being wheeled onto a hospital roof to sit in the sun? I'll tell you what excitement is. It's being alive! It's shacking up in an Armenian brothel and feeling the fleas crawling around on the bed!

MISS MADURGA. Is that what you really want?

PARMIGIAN. Yes! Fleas! I want fleas!

MISS MADURGA. (*To* LANDAU.) As you can see, Mr. Parmigian and I go back a long way.

PARMIGIAN. Yeah, six months. If you stay alive in this hospital six months, that's a long way. You become an antiquity, a pyramid of longevity.

MISS MADURGA. (*Continuing with* LANDAU. *Crosses Left to* PARMIGIAN, *tuck blanket.*) Last winter we read all five cantos of William Spenser's *Faerie Queene* together.

PARMIGIAN. Edmund Spenser!

MISS MADURGA. Yes, of course, Edmund Spenser. I'll be back in time to take you down to your appointment, Mr. Landau. (*She rests her hand gently on* PARMIGIAN's *shoulder for a moment, and then starts to exit Upstage Right.* PARMIGIAN *calls after her.*)

PARMIGIAN. It's grotesque reading the entire *Faerie Queene*, all *seven* books, and still calling him William Spenser! (*She pauses for a moment, turns around to look at him, and then exits.*) Hypocrites! Liars!

LANDAU. She seemed genuinely concerned about you.

PARMIGIAN. Oh, yeah? Well, let me tell you something. I don't need their genuine concern. All I want is the truth. You come from Puerto Rico, I don't wanna see you walking around with a diamond sticking outta your nose. You're smoking Marlboros in the broom closet, I don't wanna see you sticking up "No Smoking" signs in the corridors. No more hypocrisy! No more lies!

LANDAU. Sometimes people lie just to be kind.

PARMIGIAN. (PARMIGIAN *looks at him silently for a second.*) Jesus, you really say things like that all the time?

LANDAU. Sorry. I didn't mean to sound indifferent.

PARMIGIAN. Banal.

LANDAU. All right, banal, for whatever difference it makes. (LANDAU *stares down at the candy bar in his lap, and slowly begins re-wrapping it.* PARMIGIAN *watches him for a few moments.*)

PARMIGIAN. (*Crosses Right to* LANDAU.) What are you saving it for? Halloween? I told you it's stale.

LANDAU. I'll throw it away later. Miss Madurga gave it to me. (*Looks off Right.*) There's no garbage can out here.

PARMIGIAN. (*Reaching over and taking the candy bar out of* LANDAU's *hands.*) Don't throw it away later. (*Tosses it backward over his shoulder.*) Throw it away now.

LANDAU. (*Watching the candy bar clunk to the floor.*) I could have done that.

PARMIGIAN. Yeah, but you didn't.

LANDAU. Because it's not very neat.

PARMIGIAN. Who cares? What are you in here for anyway?

LANDAU. Exploratory surgery.

PARMIGIAN. Oh, yeah? What are they exploring for?

Cancer? (*For some reason this strikes* PARMIGIAN *as terribly funny, and he breaks out in a paroxysm of laughter.*)

LANDAU. It was just a shadow on an x-ray of my stomach, a few cells they weren't quite sure about.

PARMIGIAN. Sure.

LANDAU. Really. Just a small twinge. I don't even feel it anymore.

PARMIGIAN. Whatta ya working on, Mr. Landau?

LANDAU. I don't understand.

PARMIGIAN. Sure you understand. What are you working on? An ulcer? (PARMIGIAN *begins to laugh uncontrollably again.*) Is that what you're working on for yourself? An ulcer? You know what I thought I had? A tickle in the throat. Honest to God, that's what I thought I had. I came through the front door and I told them I had a tickle in the throat! (*The laughter stops as suddenly as it began.*) Take my word for it. On this floor it's never a twinge in the stomach. It's never a tickle in the throat. You got what I got.

LANDAU. What's that?

PARMIGIAN. The big C. You're going down for the big count, same as me, Mr. Landau, Mr. Richard Landau.

LANDAU. On the contrary, Mr. Parmigian I'm just here for exploratory surgery.

PARMIGIAN. Sure. And you're all dressed up. You look terrific in your Bloomingdale pajamas. You look . . . spiffy.

LANDAU. Thank you.

PARMIGIAN. You know what I weighed six months ago? Two hundred twenty pounds. I looked spiffy, too. I was the King Kong of the fruit and vegetable business. I had a pair of fists like two hamhocks. Now I can't even find them anymore. I tell 'em my clothing don't fit me anymore, they tell me the hospital laundry must be stretching them out. Can you believe such a pack of crap? The hospital laundry is stretching them out? You'd have to be some kind of a goddamn moron to believe something like that. What did you used to do for a living?

LANDAU. I didn't *used to* do anything for a living, Mr. Parmigian. I'm still doing it. I'm an investment advisor in Fine Art.

PARMIGIAN. Oh, yeah? What the hell's an investment advisor in Fine Art?

LANDAU. I recommend purchases in Fine Art to investors interested in capital appreciation. I generally handle accounts in European glass and Chinese ceramics.

PARMIGIAN. Hey, that's terrific. That's really terrific. You got any recommendations for long term growth? (PARMIGIAN *begins another round of uncontrollable laughter at his own joke, laughter that ends in a series of bad coughs.*)

LANDAU. Are you all right, Mr. Parmigian? Mr. Parmigian? (*When* PARMIGIAN *doesn't answer him,* LANDAU *stands out of his wheelchair, starts to cross Upstage Center.*) I'll get a nurse. I'll be right back.

PARMIGIAN. (*Grabbing his arm.*) Don't bother.

LANDAU. Are you sure you don't want me to get you somebody?

PARMIGIAN. Yes, I'm sure! I'm sure! It only hurts when I try and stay alive. When I make jokes and try and stay alive. (LANDAU *sits in wheelchair.*) Listen, as long as you're up, you wanna do me a favor?

LANDAU. If I can, yes.

PARMIGIAN. Don't worry. It's just a little favor. It's not going to put you out much.

LANDAU. What do you want me to do?

PARMIGIAN. Get behind my wheelchair and push me off the roof.

LANDAU. What?

PARMIGIAN. Get behind my wheelchair and push me off the roof. I'd do it myself only I don't have the guts.

LANDAU. I really don't think you ought to joke about something like that, Mr. Parmigian.

PARMIGIAN. You think it's a joke? (*Releasing the brake on the wheelchair.*) Look, off with the brake, off with everything. I'm ready to roll. Come on, be a sport before one of them comes out here with her morphine needle and the glucose bottle.

LANDAU. No . . . how can you ask somebody . . .

PARMIGIAN. You do it now you'll be just in time for the six o'clock news. (*Using his fingers to form an imaginary headline.*) "Incredible shrinking Armenian and his wheelchair splatter to death on the pavement in front of Hope Memorial. Cancerous dealer in Fine Art sole witness to bizarre tragedy." Listen, you'll be famous for five or six minutes.

LANDAU. (*Rises, crosses Left to* PARMIGIAN.) I have no desire to be famous at the cost of somebody else's life. Now, please, just let me put the brake . . . (*As he moves his hand toward the brake,* PARMIGIAN *slaps it away.*)

PARMIGIAN. All right. Why should I expect something for nothing. I'll make it interesting for you. As soon as you push me over I'll go into a triple somersault, a full layout, fold up like a jacknife, and do a terrific swan right through the entrance awning. You live another six months you won't see something like that again. Come on, whatta ya say?

LANDAU. I'm not going to listen to this. I don't know

whether you're joking with me or not, but I'm not going to listen to this. (*Crosses Upstage Center.*)

PARMIGIAN. All right, I'll do it myself. The railing is weak, half the screws are out. A couple of good smashes into it and over I go. (*Starts to wheel himself forward.* LANDAU *grabs his chair.*)

LANDAU. (*Locks* PARMIGIAN's *brakes.*) No!

PARMIGIAN. (*Release Right brake.*) Take your hand off my chair!

LANDAU. (*Lock Left brake.*) No, I'm not going to take my hand off your chair!

PARMIGIAN. (*Release Left brake.*) You take your hand off my chair or I'll bite it off! Do you understand me? I'll bite it off!

LANDAU. (*Lock Right brake.*) You're not going to bite anything off!

PARMIGIAN. I'm warning you, Landau! My teeth are rotten! I'll give you an infection they won't heal up with a million units of penicillin! (LANDAU *locks both brakes and stands Stage Left of* PARMIGIAN. PARMIGIAN, *suddenly losing all fight in him.*) All right. You win. I give up. I don't have the energy to fight with anybody.

LANDAU. I'm going to sit down again. You just stay where you are. Do you understand me? Right where you are. (LANDAU *sits down again in his wheelchair, keeping a wary eye on* PARMIGIAN.)

PARMIGIAN. I want a Dr. Pepper. Go inside and get me a Dr. Pepper, I'm thirsty.

LANDAU. Not now.

PARMIGIAN. What's the matter? It disturbs you?

LANDAU. Seeing somebody try to take their own life? Yes, it disturbs me. Nobody has the right to do something like that.

PARMIGIAN. Why not? Whose life is it?

LANDAU. That's not the point. The point is that
. . . Look, they're always coming up with something.

PARMIGIAN. They're coming up with nothing.

LANDAU. Don't say that because that's not true.
They're making fantastic progress all the time. Every
day you read about something new. Just last Sunday
there was an article in The Times about how cockroaches can't get cancer.

PARMIGIAN. That's wonderful news if you're a cockroach.

LANDAU. That's not the point. If they can't give
cockroaches cancer, maybe they can find out what it
is that prevents cancer.

PARMIGIAN. You want to know what prevents
cancer? Death! Death prevents cancer.

LANDAU. Well, with that attitude you might as well
just give up.

PARMIGIAN. I have. Push me off the roof.

LANDAU. Look, I can't handle this kind of thing right
now! I just . . . (*Catching himself, and then offering
up an innocuous remark in hope of ending the conversation.*) You're just depressed. Tomorrow you
won't feel so depressed, you'll be glad you're still alive.

PARMIGIAN. No, I won't.

LANDAU. Yes, you will, believe me.

PARMIGIAN. No, I won't, and why should I believe
you?

LANDAU. Because people survive! They go on! They
live. Because nobody tries to commit suicide unless
he's depressed.

PARMIGIAN. I happen to be in a very good mood at
the present moment, Mr. Landau, or hadn't you
noticed?

LANDAU. I don't call this being in a very good mood.

PARMIGIAN. Why not? The sun is shining, the grass

is coming up, the dogs are peeing all over the sidewalk. Why shouldn't I be in a very good mood?

LANDAU. You just tried to commit suicide.

PARMIGIAN. That's the best time to commit suicide, when you're in a good mood. I've tried to commit suicide three times this month, and never once was I in a bad mood.

LANDAU. You know what I think, Mr. Parmigian? I think you just enjoy the idea of committing suicide. I think if I put my hand on your wheelchair to push you off the roof, you wouldn't let me. You'd find a reason for wanting to stay alive.

PARMIGIAN. Who knows? Maybe when I got to the edge I would change my mind. You want to give it a try? You never know. (*For some long moments they stare silently at each other as if the measure of something was being taken.*)

LANDAU. Why do you insist on involving me with this? Why don't you do it yourself if you're so determined to do it?

PARMIGIAN. So the tune changes a little bit. Now you're willing to watch if you don't have to participate.

LANDAU. I didn't say that.

PARMIGIAN. I thought that was what you were saying.

LANDAU. No.

PARMIGIAN. My mistake. (*Pause.*) To tell you the truth, the reason I asked you is that I need someone to make the decision for me. I don't have the courage myself. What I said before about not having any guts is true, literal. They took out my bladder, shaved off my prostate, hooked up my large intestine to my urinary tract, and tied my bowels to my hip bone. See . . . (*Momentarily lifting up his blanket as if to expose his operation.* LANDAU *looks away.*) Now my urine flows with my blood, and when I shake my leg my liver drips prostatic fluid on my shoes. And that's the good news. You want to hear some bad news? Last week I ran outta Blue Cross. My wife tells me not to worry because I have a prosperous fruit and vegetable business in the Village. She's going to take care of my bills down to the last tangerine. That's what I'm going to leave her. These people with their x-ray machines, and their cobalt machines, and their knives and operating rooms, are going to take everything, and my wife, for thirty years of work and love, is going to be left with a tangerine. That's what I dream about at night when they give me the morphine . . . floating over the rainbow on a shrinking carpet of tangerines.

LANDAU. I'm sorry. It must be a terrible thing watching your estate being destroyed by an illness.

PARMIGIAN. It's not an estate. It's a fruit and vegetable business.

LANDAU. Yes, of course. That's what I meant.

PARMIGIAN. You believed that?

LANDAU. Believed what?

PAGMIGIAN. That I dream about floating over the rainbow on a carpet of tangerines.

LANDAU. Yes, if you say so, why not?

PARMIGIAN. Because it's a lie. Well, maybe it's not a lie, maybe it's a distortion. Actually, it's not so much a distortion as a lie—a lying distortion. That's probably the best that can be said about it. You see what state I'm in, Landau? I have no perspective. You want to know what I really dream about? Filth! Absolute filth! I pretend to myself I dream about my wife, my family, my estate, but the truth is I dream about absolute filth. A man with a shred of decency left in him wouldn't tell dreams like mine to the Marquis de Sade.

LANDAU. Fortunately, nobody's under any compunction to tell his dreams to anyone.

PARMIGIAN. You're one hundred percent right.

LANDAU. If they're medicating you with narcotics, there's no point in holding yourself responsible for your dreams.

PARMIGIAN. You are absolutely correct. No point at all. (*Pause.*) I'll tell you what, Landau. You tell me your filthy dreams and I'll tell you mine.

LANDAU. I have no dreams that would interest anybody.

PARMIGIAN. You'd be surprised at what interests me. The closer I get to death the more everything interests me. Dreams other people throw out with the garbage I can spend a whole day living on.

LANDAU. I have no dreams . . . of interest to anybody.

PARMIGIAN. What an absolutely marvellous quality of surface veneer you have, Mr. Landau.

LANDAU. If you're interested in surface veneer, perhaps I might show you something in a nineteenth century Chinese lacquer box. You might find it interesting to see how coat upon coat of lacquer can be laid down until the box itself may be removed leaving nothing behind but the form and the lacquer—the black, brilliant, slightly poisonous lacquer. (*Pause.*) I'm sorry to disappoint you, Mr. Parmigian, but there's nothing in me you're going to be able to live on. I've got nothing to give you.

PARMIGIAN. Nothing?

LANDAU. Nothing.

PARMIGIAN. All right, I'll accept that lie. There's no point in being too pushy the first ten minutes you

meet somebody. First you should break the ice, so I'll
give you an ice breaker, a riddle. What's shaped like
a big green football with four legs and a tail?

LANDAU. How outrageous you are.

PARMIGIAN. That's not the answer.

LANDAU. I don't know the answer.

PARMIGIAN. Perhaps you'd like to think about it?

LANDAU. There would be no point in thinking about
it. I don't know the answer.

PARMIGIAN. A watermelon. The answer is a watermelon.

LANDAU. A watermelon does not have four legs and
a tail.

PARMIGIAN. I lied. (*Crosses Right to* LANDAU. *For
some moments the* TWO MEN *stare silently at each
other.*) Now I'll give you the whole filthy truth. I have
a . . . dream . . . for want of a better word let's
call it a dream . . . a kind of recurrent dream which
unlike an ordinary dream, night by night, progresses
further and further, pulling me down into it—an effect
undoubtedly caused by the narcotic. In this . . .
dream, I am shacking up with a queen. (LANDAU *re-
acts slightly to the word "queen."*) Not that kind of
queen. A real queen. With a tiara on her head. She
walks around in a silk gown with her breasts almost
hanging out, and we spend our time figuring out ways
to poison her husband, the king. That surprises you,
doesn't it? You think because I own a fruit and vegetable store my imagination's limited to blueberries
and cauliflower heads.

LANDAU. I don't know what your imagination's
limited to.

PARMIGIAN. Sure you do. That's the way the mind
works. You want to be the hero of the story you've
got to look like Don Juan and Robert Redford. You

got a little defect, a pimple on your ass, and you're
out of the running, nobody wants to know you. Well,
let me tell you something. That's the same kind of
thinking we're counting on to take out the king. In
this dream, this recurrent dream that progresses night
by night, the poor bastard suffers from the same delu-
sion everybody else does. He takes one look at me
and as far as he's concerned I'm invisible. The music's
playing, and they're waltzing around in a ballroom
four thousand yards long, and I'm leaning up against
a marble pillar like a shriveled imitation of Richard
the Third—and I'm invisible. In the exalted circles of
his imperial brain, I don't exist. Well, good, okay,
because one of these nights that poor bastard's
going to be licking the sour cream off his silver spoon
and his exalted head's gonna come crashing down into
the borsch.

LANDAU. You enjoy that?

PARMIGIAN. Enjoy what?

LANDAU. Being the hero of your own dreams.

PARMIGIAN. Sure, why not? Who else should be the
hero of my dreams? Listen, maybe it's not sour cream
at all but a Charlotte Russe. How's that? Suppose it
turns out to be a poisonous maraschino cherry? A
single cough as the juice trickles down his throat,
whipped cream along the corners of his mouth . . .
and farewell, king . . . (*Noticing a strange look on*
LANDAU's *face.*) What's the matter?

LANDAU. You're talking about killing someone.

PARMIGIAN. Let me tell you about her bedroom.
Heavy red damask curtains that shut out the light of
day, a hundred pinpricks of flame from a hundred
candles glowing in little dishes of leaves and flowers
made of filigree and gold; and she moves about the

room, her reflection in the glass of a dozen smoky mirrors, the small silk butterflies on her gown making dark fluttered shadows on her perfect skin. (PARMIGIAN *has lost himself in his vision, and only slowly acknowledges* LANDAU's *presence.* PARMIGIAN *gets tooth off arm of chair. It is held there with scotch tape. He conceals it in his hand until next beat of taking tooth from mouth.*) Kill someone? I tell you, my friend, I would poison half the world to kiss a certain milk-blue vein on her breast.

LANDAU. In your dream.

PARMIGIAN. Yes, of course, in my dream. Only a madman would conceive of that awake. (*Raising his hand to his jaw and leaving out a small cry of pain.*) Ow! Ow! My teeth are rotting. They make my teeth ache in that lousy castle with their whipped creams, their cordials, their sugared strudels. Ow! Ow! (*Shaking a tooth back and forth.*)

LANDAU. You ought to see a dentist. They must have a dentist in this hospital.

PARMIGIAN. I don't need a dentist in the hospital. I need a dentist in the castle. (*Continuing to shake the tooth until he pulls it out.*) No blood. You see that? No blood at all. Dry as a dried out well. (*Rotating the tooth in his fingers.*) God, look at this tooth. A thousand facets, and every facet a filling. (*Holds up tooth and talks to it facing Stage Left.*) How many cows have we munched together? How many chickens? How many loaves of white bread? It nourished me for a lifetime, Landau, and now there's not so much as a spot of blood left in me to nourish it. Well . . . (*Throwing the tooth backwards over his head.*) So much for philosophy. What's the matter?

LANDAU. Nothing. It's just strange seeing something

that's a part of you being thrown away like that. Everything so disposable, so damn disposable.

PARMIGIAN. It's just a tooth.

LANDAU. It's still part of you . . . was part of you. Almost obscene; almost terrifying, really.

PARMIGIAN. What is?

LANDAU. A hundred dirty little jugs of oil wiped over in a hundred dirty little restaurants, and then one day you wipe away the restaurants and the people, and it's all so disposable. So here, so there, so almost never at all. (*Standing up as if suddenly reminded of something.*)

PARMIGIAN. What are you standing up for? Where are you going?

LANDAU. I have an appointment. My nurse is taking me down to the x-ray room some time this afternoon. I have to swallow something and then they're going to x-ray it.

PARMIGIAN. That's a terrific test. You'll like it a lot.

LANDAU. You had that test?

PARMIGIAN. Oh, sure. That's one of the best procedures in this hospital. That's where they wheel you in with your Bloomingdale pajamas, and when they're finished they take your pajamas away and send them to the cleaners to stretch.

LANDAU. (*Crosses Downstage Left.*) I'll be home in a few days. Time enough to finish the boiled meat in the refrigerator, time enough to have a few friends over for dinner.

PARMIGIAN. Oh, yeah, that's right. You're just in for an exploratory. I forgot. Tell me something, Landau. You seem to be in pretty good physical shape. You do something?

LANDAU. (*Crosses Right to Downstage Right of bench.*) I play squash a couple of afternoons a week, and on the weekends some tennis if I can get away.

PARMIGIAN. That's probably a big help to your whole cardiovascular system—all that movement in your Addidas sneakers.

LANDAU. Pumas. (*Crosses Downstage Left.*)

PARMIGIAN. Listen, your cardiovascular system stays in good shape there's no reason why you couldn't go on living until this time next year.

LANDAU. (*Turn Right.*) I wish you'd stop doing that.

PARMIGIAN. Doing what?

LANDAU. Implying that there's something terminal about me.

PARMIGIAN. Was that what I was doing?

LANDAU. Yes! You know perfectly well that that's . . . (*Look at watch. Crosses Upstage to Downstage of Upstage Left table, look off Right.*) oh, never mind. It doesn't make any difference.

PARMIGIAN. Tell me something, Landau. You a married man?

LANDAU. Yes.

PARMIGIAN. You got any children?

LANDAU. (*Crosses Left of bench and Downstage to below bench.*) Yes, I have two girls.

PARMIGIAN. Where do you go with your family for the summer? The end of Long Island? The Catskills?

LANDAU. Nantucket. We used to rent a house in East Hampton, but it got too . . .

PARMIGIAN. (*Interrupting him.*) It got too crowded, so you went off to Nantucket. What do you do in Nantucket? Entertain the art world and walk along the beach?

LANDAU. (*Crosses Right below PARMIGIAN.*) We get in a lot of riding. We bought some bikes.

PARMIGIAN. Ah . . . ten speed Fujis.

LANDAU. (*Sits in wheelchair.*) Peugeots.

PARMIGIAN. And you get in twenty miles of peddling with your wife every Monday, Wednesday, and Friday.

LANDAU. Weekends . . . and mostly with the kids . . . my wife prefers . . .

PARMIGIAN. (*Interrupting him again.*) Sunbathing . . . in a bikini.

LANDAU. Sunbathing in whatever she wears! You make it sound so mindless.

PARMIGIAN. Do I?

LANDAU. Yes, you do. And I don't particularly like it.

PARMIGIAN. If you're interested, I'll tell you everything there is to know about your relations with your wife.

LANDAU. You know nothing of my wife . . . not the way she boils the children's eggs, or removes the fishbones from their fish . . . nothing!

PARMIGIAN. It doesn't matter. Your wife is forty years old, maybe. She doesn't weigh any more now than when she was nineteen. When she puts on a bathing suit she's a knockout, except for the small varicose veins which you noticed just popped to the surface behind her knees last summer.

LANDAU. I think you'd better just stop right there, Mr. Parmigian.

PARMIGIAN. Why? The veins bother you?

LANDAU. Hearing you talk about my wife bothers me, that's all. (*Rises, crosses Left and Upstage Center, around Stage Right table.*)

PARMIGIAN. It annoys you she spends a couple of hundred dollars more a year on clothing than you like, but when she walks outta Bonwit Teller she looks like a million bucks, and when she stops by the office and bends over your desk she gives half the art department the hots, and that's just the way you like it . . .

LANDAU. (*Suddenly putting both his hands on the back of* PARMIGIAN'*s wheelchair.*) That's enough!

PARMIGIAN. If you don't like what I'm saying, go ahead and push me off the roof! (LANDAU *instantly leaves go of the wheelchair.*) You're a pretty violent man, Mr. Landau.

LANDAU. I'm not a violent man. You just irritated me, that's all. I've never done a violent thing in my life. I hate . . . violence. (*Walking away and staring outward at the city. Crosses Downstage Left, Stage Left of bench.*) Ugly city of gas and gasoline. City where they plant a few scraggly trees so everybody can pretend he's living back in a forest. (*Turning to* PARMIGIAN. *Crosses Right to* PARMIGIAN.) You know why these trees never grow into anything? Why they always cut them down? Because nothing is allowed to interfere with the power cables beneath the street. What has grown beautiful on the surface must not offend the thrust of power below the surface. That's when the city comes. (*Crosses Left to Downstage Left chair.*) One morning in my sleep I hear power saws— buzz, buzz—men with uniforms, hands like brown leather. "Why are you cutting down those trees?" "Mind your own business, Jack! Stick your head back in your window, Jack!" A week later they're back again. Six holes the size of a dog's grave are dug, and they plant the replacements—trees no thicker than a broomstick. (*Crosses to* PARMIGIAN *at Center Stage.*) For thirty years a tree is allowed to live, cut into by children with penknives, shit on by dogs, backed into by cars, allowed to grow into something of dignity and value—to be replaced by a broomstick? There is no replacement! What is killed is killed forever! (*Crosses Left to Stage Left of bench.*)

PARMIGIAN. Listen, it doesn't pay to get irritated. You'll probably be back on the squash court in two or three weeks.

LANDAU. You think so?

PARMIGIAN. No.

LANDAU. (*Turns Right.*) What the devil's the matter with you?

PARMIGIAN. That's pretty obvious, isn't it?

LANDAU. I'm not talking about that. You don't seem to give an ounce of thought to what you're saying. I don't know you ten minutes and you got the gall to talk to me as if you've known me for ten years. (*Crosses Down to Downstage of bench.*) You don't know anything about me, my family, or my wife.

PARMIGIAN. That's right.

LANDAU. You bet that's right. So let's just knock it off.

PARMIGIAN. I apologize.

LANDAU. All right. Let's just forget it. (*Crosses Right below* PARMIGIAN *to Stage Right table, gets magazine.*)

PARMIGIAN. I can see you're a very private person.

LANDAU. (*Crosses Downstage to wheelchair. Puts on glasses.*) All right. All right. Let's just forget it. (PARMIGIAN *crosses Stage Left and Downstage Right of bench.*)

PARMIGIAN. (*After some moments of silence.*) Landau? (*Turns Downstage, move Stage Left to Downstage Right of bench.*)

LANDAU. What?

PARMIGIAN. Are you of the Hebrew persuasion?

LANDAU. Yes, I'm Jewish. What about it?

PARMIGIAN. Nothing.

LANDAU. Then why did you bring it up?

PARMIGIAN. I just wanted you to know . . . some of my best friends are Jewish.

LANDAU. (*Pause.* PARMIGIAN *moves Stage Left Center. Staring at him.*) That's . . . wonderful. That's just . . . beautiful.

PARMIGIAN. To tell you the truth I'm beginning to lose my friends.

LANDAU. I wonder why.

PARMIGIAN. Don't wonder why! You'll find out. At the beginning you get a lot of friends dropping in . . . two, three dozen of them a day . . . and then after a while it drops off. They don't come around anymore. You're lucky to get a handful of drooping flowers once a month. You know what those miserable drooping flowers remind me of?

LANDAU. (*Closing his eyes and resting his fingers against them.*) No. But I have a feeling you're going to tell me.

PARMIGIAN. A vision I used to have when I was a young man. It was a vision of immortal ripeness, a summer's day when time stopped and everything was frozen into its exact moment of perfection. The peaches were hanging perfectly on every tree, every blade of grass was perfectly formed into a little tiny green spear . . . I was a grasshopper setting out for a day of love through an endless field of strawberries . . . (PARMIGIAN *just breaks off without finishing.*)

LANDAU. (*Opening his eyes.*) And then what?

PARMIGIAN. And then what? Time began. The grasshopper took a big leap and got hit with a spray of D.D.T.

LANDAU. If you're that interested in frozen perfection, Mr. Parmigian, maybe you ought to visit the deep freeze at Food City.

PARMIGIAN. Ah, you're coming back to life: a little sarcasm, a little insensitivity. Maybe you'll understand what I'm trying to tell you as well. You married your wife as I married my wife, expecting eternal perfection.

LANDAU. That's not why I married my wife.

PARMIGIAN. Wasn't it?

LANDAU. No. What you're talking about is a parody of love, some kind of grotesque parody.

PARMIGIAN. Then why is it the veins in the back of her legs are beginning to bother you?

LANDAU. They don't bother me! What bothers me is a man who talks about love and perfection and obviously understands neither. You're in love, Mr. Parmigian, you don't stand around examining someone for physical deterioration.

PARMIGIAN. I do. (LANDAU *turn Downstage Right to edge of Stage.*) You see what Time is, Landau? Everyman's Launcelot reaches Everyman's Lady in the Lake only to find out that she's turned into Mother Cabrini.

LANDAU. Maybe your wife looks like Mother Cabrini, but not mine.

PARMIGIAN. My wife's a saint, that's why she looks the way she does. But that's not here or there, either. The point is that Everyman, you, me, Don Quixote, Everyman, spends his life in a fevered quest for the unattainable, the object desired beyond belief: The Lady in the Lake, the Holy Grail, the Moon Goddess on the Mountain, whatever you wish; but even as we get there, even as the object of our quest is finally in our hand, at that ultimate moment of exaltation, what happens? The object diminishes, it turns meaningless in front of us, it disappears in our hand like a crystal of snow. Don't you find that odd, Landau? Don't you find that very odd?

LANDAU. I don't find it anything. I never really thought about it.

PARMIGIAN. No great quests in your life?

LANDAU. No.

PARMIGIAN. No great adventures?

LANDAU. (*Turn Stage Left.*) I buy art for people interested in capital appreciation. Twice a week if I can get away I play squash. Mornings I drink my coffee, afternoons I bite into a sandwich. That's my great adventure.

PARMIGIAN. (*Crosses above* LANDAU *to Stage Right.*) Oh, what a great liar you are. Death is knocking like a recruiting officer on the front door, and you still persist in lying to yourself.

LANDAU. I've never lied to myself about anything. I've never had the luxury.

PARMIGIAN. Bullshit! It's time to stop fencing with me, Landau! It is time for you to spread your filthy dream out in front of me like a moth eaten Moroccan carpet!

LANDAU. I don't have any filthy dreams, and even if I did I don't see how you could be interested in sexual perversions in the condition you're in. (*Turn Stage Left, crosses 2' Stage Left, lock brakes.*)

PARMIGIAN. (*His voice gradually rising with fanatical zeal.*) I'm not talking about sexual perversions. I wouldn't give two cents for the pathetically harmless sexual imaginings of your Jewish brain. What I'm talking about is the will-o'-the-wisp you've been pursuing all your life, the loadstone, the magnetic star that pulls you and all of us through all the years of our life, attracts us though we hate it; that's the real pornography of our brain, the one common central lie that sits at the heart of all our lives, distorting it, corrupting it, deforming it! It is this lie, and this lie alone, that is the enduring filth of our lives!

LANDAU. (*Grown equally excited.*) What lie? What lie are you talking about?

PARMIGIAN. (*Suddenly calm.*) I haven't got the faintest idea. I thought you might know. You're Jewish.

LANDAU. What has that got to do with anything?

PARMIGIAN. Everybody knows Jews are filled with secrets, all kinds of oriental cabala nobody knows anything about.

LANDAU. (*Rises, putting magazine on table, shove wheelchair, crosses Upstage to Upstage Left table.*) That's garbage! Absolute garbage!

PARMIGIAN. You deny it?

LANDAU. (*Paces around bench, counterclockwise.*) Yes, of course I deny it!

PARMIGIAN. Naturally, of course. I can see I made a mistake with you. I should have passed myself off as a Jew, then we'd be having a different sort of discussion out here. We wouldn't be engaged in pleasant chit chat. We'd be talking about the mysteries of the universe, things of importance that have been kept secret for five thousand years. Unfortunately, we're never going to be discussing this because I revealed myself to you as an Arab!

LANDAU. I thought you were from Armenia? You said you were from Armenia!

PARMIGIAN. That's close enough to being an Arab! And while we're on the subject of Arabs, let me tell you the only ones in the world that really understand Jews are those with Arabian blood in them like me! There's something flowing through Arabian blood that lets us understand Jews!

LANDAU. (*Crosses Downstage to below bench, level with* PARMIGIAN.) What? Camel dung? What are you talking about? The only thing flowing through blood is blood cells!

PARMIGIAN. (*Crosses Left to Downstage Right of bench.*) You don't believe in racial memories? You think after five thousand years of Arabs and Jews living together the secrets of one don't flow in the blood of the other?

LANDAU. (PARMIGIAN *chases* LANDAU *around bench, counterclock and Downstage Right.* PARMIGIAN *reaches Center Stage.*) There are no secrets! There's nothing there to flow!

PARMIGIAN. Don't tell me what flows and what doesn't flow! You've got a secret! Every Jew's got a secret! Why don't you do yourself a favor and get the filthy thing off your chest once and for all? (LANDAU *turns and crosses Left to Downstage Right of table.* PARMIGIAN *stops.*) Look at it this way: sooner or later you're going to spill your guts out here, everybody does; maybe you'll call in a rabbi and what do you (LANDAU *crosses Right to lamp.*) think he's going to do with what you tell him? He's gonna tell it to his wife, and inside of two seconds it's going to be all over the congregation. You won't be able to eat a piece of matzoh without having half a dozen bearded faces staring at you. With me you get a guarantee. Where I'm going nobody brings messages back from.

LANDAU. (*Turn Left.*) What is that? A guarantee? You're going to give me a guarantee?

PARMIGIAN. Absolutely. I know my customers. You buy the suit you get a guarantee and two pairs of pants.

LANDAU. (*Crosses Left to below chair Stage Left of*

Stage Right table.) What the hell is that supposed to mean?

PARMIGIAN. With a Jew you give him a guarantee; if you were a Puerto Rican I'd give you a bunch of dominoes.

LANDAU. What an incredibly bigoted thing that is to say!

PARMIGIAN. You think I'm a bigot?

LANDAU. Yes, I think you're a bigot! Yes!

PARMIGIAN. Where do you get the nerve to accuse me of being a bigot? Let me tell you something. I happen to be a member of The American Civil Liberties Union. You can't be a bigot and be a member of The American Civil Liberties Union.

LANDAU. (*Crosses Left to confront* PARMIGIAN.) Then don't talk that way! I wasn't out here five minutes before you were making comments about my nurse because she's from Puerto Rico according to you, and then you're making anti-Semitic statements to me about being a Jew and needing a guarantee, and then you're back on the Puerto Ricans with their dominoes!

PARMIGIAN. That's what they do. They play dominoes. What's the matter? You don't see them on the street playing dominoes?

LANDAU. That's not what I'm talking about. It's the implications of what you're saying. I'm a Jew so I need a guarantee. What is that supposed to mean? A Jew is tight fisted with his money? He's different than anybody else? You know, I don't believe I'm having this conversation! I don't believe I've gotten myself involved in a conversation like this! (*Crosses Right to below Stage Right table.*)

PARMIGIAN. What makes you so touchy?

LANDAU. I'm not touchy!

PARMIGIAN. Listen, Landau, take my word for it. You're touchy. It's very difficult holding a pleasant conversation with you.

LANDAU. Then stop making those kind of remarks! I've heard them all before.

PARMIGIAN. Oh, yeah? Where was that?

LANDAU. (*Crosses Upstage to Stage Right rail.*) What difference does it make where? It doesn't make any difference where!

PARMIGIAN. What's the matter? That's another secret, too? I never met a man with so many secrets. Talking to you is like talking to a sphinx: the tongue sits in the mouth without a word while the feet are being eaten up with the sand. (LANDAU *crosses Left above table to* PARMIGIAN.)

LANDAU. I'd like to see that card.

PARMIGIAN. What card?

LANDAU. The one from The American Civil Liberties Union.

PARMIGIAN. What's the matter? You don't think I'm a member of The American Civil Liberties Union? Let me tell you something. I marched in three separate peace marches! I was there when the draft cards were burned! I was there when it took real courage to stand up for what you believed in!

LANDAU. Just let me see the card.

PARMIGIAN. I was singing "Blowing in the Wind," and the F.B.I. was taking pictures!

LANDAU. Just let me see the card.

PARMIGIAN. You want to see the card?

LANDAU. Yes! Yes! I want to see the card!

PARMIGIAN. Then I will show it to you, Mister, Mister Dealer in Fine Arts for investment purposes. I've got it right here in my pajama pocket because I can't leave my wallet in my room because of the Puerto Ricans. (*Pulling out his wallet and irately flipping through a stack of cards.*) You want a card? I will show you a card! (*Pulls out a card and tosses it at* LANDAU.) There's a membership card! (LANDAU *picks it up.*) Now what do you have to say for yourself?

LANDAU. This is a membership card in the B'nai B'rith.

PARMIGIAN. So what? I'm a member of that, too. You want cards? I'll show you cards. (*Begins wildly tossing cards at* LANDAU.) Here's one from the Police Athletic League. And here's one from the March of Dimes and Ralph Nader and the Japanese Dragon Society, and a credit card from what's left of Abercrombie and Fitch . . .

LANDAU. (*Being inundated with cards.*) Never mind! Never mind!

PARMIGIAN. (*Continuing with all the zeal of the truly offended man.*) And a membership card from the time I worked in The International Ladies Garment Workers!

LANDAU. I said never mind! Forget it!

PARMIGIAN. You want cards? I got cards! Don't you tell me what I belong to. I was a member of the American Indian Society when they couldn't sell a blanket by a railroad station! You come into my room I'll show you a real Navajo blanket hanging from the wall!

LANDAU. All right. All right.

PARMIGIAN. I happen to have a personal letter from Sacco and Vanzetti!

LANDAU. All right!

PARMIGIAN. I had a correspondence with a Rosen-

bergs! (LANDAU *shoves cards at* PARMIGIAN.) Watch
out for my urine bag! I don't want to sit here like an
old man with stains on his legs! (LANDAU *crosses Right,
sits in wheelchair facing Stage Right.*)

LANDAU. (*Turn Left.*) What are you doing with a
B'nai B'rith card?

PARMIGIAN. Why shouldn't I have a B'nai B'rith
card? I support everything! Everything has a right
to live.

LANDAU. (*Standing.*) Not everything. (*Rises, Downstage Left. Walks over to the edge and stares outward.*)

PARMIGIAN. What's the matter now? You remembered another appointment?

LANDAU. No.

PARMIGIAN. I touched another nerve?

LANDAU. You touched nothing.

PARMIGIAN. Then why are you in and out of your
chair, Jack in the Box?

LANDAU. I just don't like sitting in it, that's all.

PARMIGIAN. Why not? It's a terrific looking chair.

LANDAU. Look, maybe it's a terrific looking chair to
you, but it's not a terrific looking chair to me. I . . .
I don't like the feeling of being tied down to it.
(*Crosses Downstage Right looking out.*)

PARMIGIAN. So who's tying you down to it? Just
because your nurse put you in a wheelchair doesn't
mean you have to sit in it. It's just a hospital regula-
tion to wheel you around from place to place so you
can get used to being a cripple.

LANDAU. There's a surgical supply store across the
street. The cab left me out in front of it yesterday.
A whole window full of trusses, artificial arms and
legs, perfect plastic arms and legs hanging in the

window, stacked up on little shelves like pieces of cordwood.

PARMIGIAN. Let me tell you something. A good truss is a terrific thing. (*Throwing back his blanket.*) I can show you a truss here . . .

LANDAU. Never mind! I don't want to see it.

PARMIGIAN. What's the matter, Mr. Landau? You don't like broken things? Let me tell you, everything gets broken. Nothing stays in one piece forever. Not even a grasshopper sitting on a strawberry.

LANDAU. A good piece of ceramic does; a good piece of porcelain with a fine underglaze. I picked up a pair of Kwan-yin figures made out of blanc de chine at an estate auction last month. They were absolutely perfect without that slightly green color you see so often in even the best of white porcelain. The man I bought them for wanted to know if he could drill a small hole through the bottom so he could run an electric cord up through it. He thought they would make a fine pair of lamps.

PARMIGIAN. So what did you tell him?

LANDAU. (*After a long moment of silence.*) I told him he could do what he wanted with them. (*There's another long moment of silence before* PARMIGIAN *answers.*)

PARMIGIAN. Well . . . sometimes you need a good lamp in the house.

LANDAU. (*Spinning around to face* PARMIGIAN.) Not out of Kwan-yin figures! Not out of two hundred years of . . . of . . . (*Backstage Left.*)

PARMIGIAN. Perfection?

LANDAU. Yes. Perfection.

PARMIGIAN. Everything ends up being made into something else. When I first got married, I had an orange crate. You know what I made it into? A coffee table. It was also a dog house because the dog used to creep in from the side and sleep in it. (LANDAU *walks away in annoyance.* PARMIGIAN *watches him pace around a bit before coming to a halt in front on the flower box.*) You like that? That's the spring garden. It's also the winter, summer, fall garden, because they never take it out of there.

LANDAU. It almost looks alive until you touch it.

PARMIGIAN. It's better than alive. It's plastic. You hose it down every once in a while you'd think you were in the Garden of Eden. (*Pause.*)

LANDAU. How unpleasant a forgery is when you expected life. (*Crosses Upstage Right.*)

PARMIGIAN. Or you could sit here and look out and imagine you're on a big sailing ship. (LANDAU *crosses Upstage Center.*) You want to be a navigator, Landau? Forget about your pots and pans, and I'll make you into a navigator. You see that building over there? (LANDAU *turns Downstage.*) That's the North Star. I say that's the North Star because you never want to look up for the real North Star, because that's where the seagulls are. I was sitting right here with and ice cream cone and one of them went right on it. He took off from the East River and made a direct hit from forty thousand feet.

LANDAU. That what you do? Sit here all the time? (*Crosses Downstage to Right Center level with* PARMIGIAN.)

PARMIGIAN. Why should I sit here all the time? I've got a busy schedule for myself. Before breakfast I sit in my room. After breakfast I sit by the nurses' station. (LANDAU *crosses Downstage Left below bench.*) There's also another spot you can sit. The dayroom. There's a woman in the dayroom who sits there with a pack of cards. She's a bridge player waiting for three customers who can sit up straight in a chair. In my frank opinion the statistical probability of this happening is from nil to nothing, but this woman is a survivor from the Titanic or the Hudson River Day Line—whichever one—the story is never clear from her. If you want, I'll introduce you.

LANDAU. No, thank you.

PARMIGIAN. Smart move on your part because two months ago she spilled a bottle of Pepsi-Cola on the table and made a big mess for herself: the napkin was stuck to the table, the cards were stuck to the cards—it was a big mess. She spent all morning crying about it, but you can't play with cards like that.

LANDAU. That's your busy schedule?

PARMIGIAN. I get them on the rounds, too.

LANDAU. What rounds? What are you talking about?

PARMIGIAN. (*Turn Left to* LANDAU.) The old doctors come around with the young doctors every day, and if your case has some interest for them, they stand around your bed making suggestions. I'll tell you one thing, Landau: make yourself interesting the night before they make up the schedule. Make sure they put you down on the list. Don't let them pass you by. (*Briefly glancing backward to make sure they're alone.*) You know what I got? A PDR. You know what a PDR is? (LANDAU *shakes his head.*) A PDR is a Physician's Desk Reference. I bought it from an intern for five dollars. You know what a PDR has? It lists all the reactions to the drugs. So what I do when they give me a drug is I develop a new reaction, a reaction they can't find in the PDR. This makes my case interesting. (MISS MADURGA *enters and goes over to* LANDAU.)

MISS MADURGA. They should be ready for you now

in x-ray, Mr. Landau. (MISS MADURGA *crosses Downstage to Stage Right of* LANDAU *wheelchair.*)

LANDAU. All right. Thank you.

MISS MADURGA. I'll take you in your chair, please. (LANDAU *stops, crosses Downstage to chair and* MISS MADURGA *wheels him to Upstage Center above Stage Left edge of rail.* MISS MADURGA *takes an ice-cream sandwich out of the pocket of her uniform, the kind of ice-cream sandwich that comes from a machine, and hands it to* PARMIGIAN. *He takes it wordlessly, staring at her.*) I had it left over from lunch. I don't know why I bought it. (MISS MADURGA *crosses Upstage.*)

PARMIGIAN. Have a good afternoon, Landau. (*The* NURSE *starts to wheel* LANDAU *off Right when* PARMIGIAN *shouts after him.*) Remember what I said to you! Be interesting! (*They exit.* PARMIGIAN, *staring down at the ice-cream sandwich he holds in his lap, speaks softly to himself.*) Be interesting. (*LIGHTS fade out.*)

END OF ACT ONE

ACT TWO

The roof garden. Early evening of the same day.

ON RISE: PARMIGIAN, *Stage Left in his wheelchair, leafs through a newspaper.* LANDAU, *seated now Stage Right in a nearby lounge chair, stares mutely down at his hands. For some moments, as* PARMIGIAN *studies the T.V. section, all is silence.*

PARMIGIAN. Everything's a re-run. Eight o'clock is a re-run, nine o'clock is a re-run, the Movie of the Week is a re-run. June is a month filled with contempt.

LANDAU. How can you watch that junk?

PARMIGIAN. That's my weakness, Landau. Everything interests me. Even junk.

LANDAU. What happened to all your reading? I thought you used to read all the time.

PARMIGIAN. I read everything already. Shakespeare, Spenser, Chaucer. Marlowe, Gunga Din. If you want to know the truth, I'm the only person in the world who ever read *The Faerie Queene* twice. The second time was a re-run. You want the newspaper?

LANDAU. No, thank you.

PARMIGIAN. You should read the newspaper. Keep up an interest in world events. (*Throws the newspaper away on the floor.*) It's better than staring down at candy wrappers or your fingernails. What are you looking for down there? A hangnail?

LANDAU. (*Putting on a pair of reading glasses.*) I was just thinking about something, that's all.

40

PARMIGIAN. Don't think. It's a waste of time. Whatever there is in this world to think about has already been thought about. (LANDAU *opens up a leather attache case and begins studying a folder full of papers.*) You know what Spengler said after he got done thinking about *The Decline of the West?* "I got a headache." The same thing was said by Hegel. The same thing was said by Schopenhauer. The same thing was said by all of them with the exception of Plato. With him it was a slightly different story. He got a wet behind from sitting too much in a cave. What happened with your x-rays?

LANDAU. Nothing. It was inconclusive.

PARMIGIAN. And you expected results. Let me tell you something. In this hospital there are no results. Everything is always inconclusive. Even the food is inconclusive. It looked like a piece of veal on my plate tonight, but when I pushed away the gravy it looked like a piece of pork, except when I took a bite of it, it tasted like turkey. So what was it?

LANDAU. Well, what did you order? You must have ordered something.

PARMIGIAN. Ice cream.

LANDAU. I mean for the main course.

PARMIGIAN. That's what I ordered for the main course. Ice cream.

LANDAU. You can't live on ice cream, Mr. Parmigian.

PARMIGIAN. Sure you can live on ice cream. There was once a famous emperor who lived on nothing but ice cream. That's what he was called, the Emperor of Ice Cream. Except for an occasional rotten tooth, he was doing okay for himself.

LANDAU. (*Matter-of-factly, as he makes a note on one of his pages.*) Nobody lives on ice cream.

PARMIGIAN. (*Suddenly, almost inexplicably, reacting violently.*) Don't tell me nobody lives on ice cream! If you want to live on ice cream, you can live on ice cream! For your information there happens to be a tribe of savages in Borneo that lives on nothing but sweet potatoes! If you can live on sweet potatoes, you can live on ice cream. And when I am finished with the ice cream, if all I can eat is chocolate mousse, then I am going to live on chocolate mousse! (LANDAU *crosses Downstage to table with papers. Pause. They exchange looks,* LANDAU *turns back to work.* PARMIGIAN's *outburst results in an embarrassed silence for both* MEN.) You want to hear something interesting? During the war I worked for a man who used to wear a white apron and had eyes like a lizard. He taught me everything there was to know about the fruit and vegetable business, and now, for the last three days, I can't remember what the rest of his face looks like. (LANDAU *sits in chair Stage Left of Stage Right table.* LANDAU *remains occupied with his work, refusing to be pulled into conversation.*) What are you working on there?

LANDAU. Some items coming up for sale in an estate auction.

PARMIGIAN. What interests you?

LANDAU. Some nineteenth century glass, and some Japanese bronzes.

PARMIGIAN. What else interests you?

LANDAU. I might put in a bid on some Cheret lithographs.

PARMIGIAN. Who's Cheret?

LANDAU. He made posters . . . a contemporary of Toulouse-Lautrec.

PARMIGIAN. You got anything going for you in the twentieth century, Landau?

LANDAU. Not in this auction.

PARMIGIAN. Besides this auction.

LANDAU. (*Suddenly stops shuffling through his papers, and sits still.*) Besides this auction I don't know what you mean, Mr. Parmigian.

PARMIGIAN. Why is it, Landau, I always get the feeling you know exactly what I mean, but you're always telling me you don't know what I mean? (LANDAU *removes his glasses and looks up, as if he might say something.*) You like cuckoo clocks, Landau?

LANDAU. Not particularly. Why do you ask me that?

PARMIGIAN. I used to have a German cuckoo clock. It kept terrific time, except after a while the cuckoo stopped coming out.

LANDAU. So?

PARMIGIAN. So what?

LANDAU. So what is the point?

PARMIGIAN. What point? There is no point. I just wanted to tell you what happened to my cuckoo clock. (LANDAU, *slightly irritated, stares at him for a moment, and then puts his glasses back on again, and returns to work.*) You ever make a mistake with what you're doing, Landau?

LANDAU. Everybody makes mistakes.

PARMIGIAN. What was your biggest mistake?

LANDAU. I don't remember offhand. I'm really rather busy here, Mr. Parmigian.

PARMIGIAN. You don't remember your biggest mistake?

LANDAU. (*Turns to* PARMIGIAN.) I bought an engraving by Pieter Bruegel that turned out to have been done by Van der Heyden.

PARMIGIAN. Van der Heyden. That sounds like a big mistake.

LANDAU. It was. (*Turns back to work.*)

PARMIGIAN. I made a big mistake like that once. I thought it was going to be a big summer for pomegranates. (LANDAU *turns to* PARMIGIAN.) I bought two hundred pomegranates and a hundred and six of them rotted.

LANDAU. Pomegranates? How can you talk about pomegranates when I'm talking to you about Pieter Bruegel.

PARMIGIAN. Why not? What's the difference? A mistake is a mistake.

LANDAU. There's no difference in your mind between an engraving by Pieter Bruegel and a bunch pomegranates?

PARMIGIAN. Sure there's a difference. One's a painter, and the other's a pomegranate.

LANDAU. (*Rises, Backstage Left.*) And that's the difference?

PARMIGIAN. That's right. That's the difference.

LANDAU. I'm not going to argue this. (*Sits in chair Stage Left of Stage Right table. Returning to his work.*)

PARMIGIAN. (*Crosses Right above table to Stage Right.*) What's the matter? I don't have enough culture for you? Let me tell you something. There was a great culture in Armenia when the Jews in Egypt didn't know how to put up a ten foot pyramid! When the Greeks were walking around without underwear, they were making rugs in Armenia with a thousand knots to the inch!

LANDAU. That has nothing to do with the difference between a Bruegel and a pomegranate! We were talking about Bruegel and pomegranates!

PARMIGIAN. I know what we were talking about!

LANDAU. Then what is your point? What is your point, Mr. Parmigian?

PARMIGIAN. What are you getting your eyes all clouded up for? You look like you got a thunderstorm in your face.

LANDAU. (*Rises.*) I want to know your point! What is your point?

PARMIGIAN. My point is that when you consider a cuckoo clock that keeps time without a cuckoo, when you can work all those years for a man who walked around with a white apron and had eyes like a lizard and still can't remember his face, when *you* can make a mistake with a painting, and *I* can make a mistake with a hundred and six pomegranates . . . (PARMIGIAN, *his voice reaching a crescendo of intensity, suddenly comes to an abrupt stop.*)

LANDAU. Yes? What?

PARMIGIAN. I don't know. I forgot the point. There was a point, but I forgot what it was.

LANDAU. Then what are you yelling about? How can you scream about everything with such conviction when you don't even know the point of what you're talking about?

PARMIGIAN. (*Crosses below table to Left Center level with Downstage edge of bench.*) Because I know something that nobody else in the world knows.

LANDAU. What? What do you know?

PARMIGIAN. I know the secret of the universe! (*Turns Right to face* LANDAU.) The same secret the Jewish rabbis were working on in their secret cabalas for the last five thousand years!

LANDAU. What secret? And don't start in with the Jews again. I've heard enough about Jews from Gentiles to last me ten lifetimes. (*Sits.*)

PARMIGIAN. What have you heard?

LANDAU. Never mind what I've heard. Just stick to the point. What secret of the universe?

PARMIGIAN. *The* secret of the universe! *The* secret! The one and only secret worth a damn! It came to me one summer night when I was alone in the store. My last customer, a midget, had just left and I was staring down at a hundred and six rotten plantains. You know what a plantain is?

LANDAU. Yes.

PARMIGIAN. It's a big banana.

LANDAU. I know what a plantain is . . . and I thought it was a hundred and six pomegranates. That's what you were talking about before, wasn't it? Pomegranates!

PARMIGIAN. The pomegranates were from the year before. This time it was plantains, a hundred and six of them. Staring down, looking at that rotten fruit, I asked myself what is the purpose behind creating fruit whose only reason for existence is to rot? That's when I heard the voice. The voice said to me, "You're missing the point, Parmigian. The point is, there is no point! And while you're at it you ought to stop by the hospital and check out that tickle in your throat." And that, my friend, my Jewish friend, is the secret of the universe. There is no point! I, Joseph Parmigian, have solved the problem five thousand rabbis with five thousand beards working five thousand years couldn't solve—there is no point! (*Turn Downstage Left. For a long moment there is silence between the two* MEN, *and then* PARMIGIAN *sticks his hand into his robe pocket and withdraws a piece of cake neatly wrapped in a napkin. With great precision he carefully folds back each of the four corners of the napkin, exposing the cake.*) You want a piece of hospital rum cake? It's made without rum.

LANDAU. (*Ignoring the offer.*) There is a point to

things in this world. Just because you haven't found it,
doesn't mean it isn't there.

PARMIGIAN. (*Biting into his cake.*) Good. Good.
Maybe you'll tell me what it is?

LANDAU. I don't have to tell you. All you have to do
is look around you.

PARMIGIAN. (*Idly looking around.*) Where should I
look?

LANDAU. Not under your wheelchair, Mr. Parmigian.
There's a sky over your head, a universe. You look
at it and then tell me there's no point to it.

PARMIGIAN. (*Staring at the sky for some moments.*)
There's no point to it.

LANDAU. Forget it. I don't have the time for this.
(*Trying to return to his work.*)

PARMIGIAN. Sure you have the time. You got at least
six months. You want to see some real action, Landau?
Look under my wheelchair. There's an ant carrying
off a dead roach. And there comes his buddy. He's
going to help him carry off the roach, and later the
both of them are going to come back and finish off
the crumbs from the rum cake.

LANDAU. You turn everything into meaninglessness,
don't you?

PARMIGIAN. Don't overestimate me, Landau. Some
days I can't even turn my wheelchair. I want to come
out here I have to sit by my door, waiting for some
jerk to come along and give me a push. And sometimes they even forget I'm out here. It rains and I sit
out here, screaming my head off for half an hour and
nobody hears me. So I sit here waiting . . . waiting
for what? A push inside? No, not a push inside. I am
waiting for something . . . something!

LANDAU. (*Speaking almost to himself, almost as if
it just slipped out.*) The courage to die.

PARMIGIAN. (*Turning to him.*) What did you say?

LANDAU. It's unimportant. I was thinking of something else . . . someone else.

PARMIGIAN. Don't tell me it's unimportant. You said something. What was it?

LANDAU. I said you were probably waiting for the courage to die. I'm sorry. I didn't mean it the way it sounded.

PARMIGIAN. Don't be sorry. It's a very good observation. "Waiting for the courage to die." It shows a brain with a lot of perception. Unfortunately, that's not what I'm waiting for. (LANDAU *looks at watch.*) What time is it now on your five hundred dollar Rolex?

LANDAU. (*Crosses to Upstage Left table.*) A quarter after seven. (*Pours himself a cup of tea and picks up a catalogue.*)

PARMIGIAN. You know what happens in another fifteen minutes? The midget I told you about with a moustache and a Brooks Brothers' suit comes into my store. The beginning of every week he comes in for an artichoke and a little plastic bag of dried up oriental mushrooms. For six years I waited for him to tell me what kind of a dish it is he makes from an artichoke and a bag of dried up oriental mushrooms.

LANDAU. (*Crosses Downstage Left.*) Why don't you ask him? If you're so interested why don't you just ask him? (*Sits in Downstage Left chair, reading catalogue.*)

PARMIGIAN. Because that's what he's waiting for! Why should I give him the satisfaction? He stands there by the cash register with a crooked smile and a little leather Gucci briefcase in his hand . . . sometimes with a cigar, too, puffing smoke rings big as a garbage can cover. What happened to your private duty nurse?

LANDAU. She left at four o'clock.

PARMIGIAN. She's coming back tomorrow?

LANDAU. No. I won't need a private duty nurse until after the exploratory.

PARMIGIAN. Ask for the same one.

LANDAU. Why? What difference does it make?

PARMIGIAN. You know what a toad looks like, Landau? You don't get that one back, they'll give you a toad.

LANDAU. I thought you didn't like her. You said she was too fat.

PARMIGIAN. (*Answering with some difficulty.*) She used to sit on the edge of my bed, reading to me in a thin dress with the sunlight coming through . . . driving me crazy. (*Looking directly at* LANDAU.) Now she got engaged to a man who eats plantains, and her dress is as thick as a rubber sheet. (*Noticing a change of expression on* LANDAU's *face.*) What's the matter, Mr. Landau. You don't think I have a penis anymore? I'll give you a surprise. I got a penis! In spite of all the operations, and the cutting, and the needles, and the twisting around, I got a penis. And when it comes time for me to leave this hospital, I'm going out like a knight from the *Faerie Queene*—with everything I got sticking straight up in the air! (*The lights on the roof garden come on automatically.*) That's the warning light. It comes on automatically. Impending darkness sensed without benefit of human intelligence. (PARMIGIAN *seems to have a little trouble breathing now.*) In half an hour the new tenants of this place arrive. Four hundred thousand mosquitoes from Flushing—my visitors for the evening. They're crossing the East River right now.

LANDAU. Why don't you give yourself a break, Mr. Parmigian? You look exhausted.

PARMIGIAN. You getting any visitors tonight?

LANDAU. No. My wife'll be here tomorrow with the children.

PARMIGIAN. What about your parents? Your friends from the world of ceramics and cut glass?

LANDAU. I'm not expecting any visitors.

PARMIGIAN. You're a smart man, Landau. A man without expectations. A realist. You know what happens to friends? They vanish like a row of chicken hawks taking off from a branch. They used to come around with flowers . . . they bought them in the subway, but a flower's a flower . . . they used to come around in the afternoon, in the evening. Then when the ultimate prognosis was made, they could hardly wait to get out of here. Two seconds in the room and they'd start fidgeting, looking at the ceiling, looking at the walls. I'd lie there looking at what? A tiny ant, once, that had climbed eighteen stories up from the street just to frizzle to death on the radiator. And then they'd leave, rushing out into the street with their hangman faces, disappearing into the traffic like a puff of smoke.

LANDAU. People do for us what they can.

PARMIGIAN. That's a brilliant perception, Landau. You know what I'm going to do with it as soon as I leave this roof? I'm going to write it down in my book of Great Sayings of the Western World.

LANDAU. (*Rises, crosses Upstage to Upstage Left table, set cup. Crosses Stage Right to above table, leave catalogue on Downtage Left urn.*) It doesn't help anything being unpleasant, Mr. Parmigian.

PARMIGIAN. Another great saying from the man without expectations. For your information everything in this hospital is improved by being unpleasant. You know what a semi-private room is when you're pleasant? It's four in a room. You know what a semi-private room is when you're unpleasant? It's yourself in a room!

LANDAU. (*Crosses to Upstage of Stage Right table, take grey catalogue.*) And that's what you like? Being alone?

PARMIGIAN. Sure, that's what I like. Now I don't have to listen to people with appendectomies, people with prostatectomies, people with stones, and nose jobs, and one with a pacemaker in his heart buzzing away with atomic energy at four in the morning. Now I can concentrate totally on my disease. I can devote my entire thought process to my disease—which happens to be the emperor of disease! The emperor!

LANDAU. (*Crosses to Right Center, Stage Right of* PARMIGIAN.) If that's the way you feel, why do you work out such a busy social schedule for yourself: nine o'clock by the nursing station, ten o'clock hustling back into bed to catch the doctors on their rounds, eleven o'clock out here? That's a little bit inconsistent, isn't it?

PARMIGIAN. One thing has nothing to do with the other. It's a matter of respect.

LANDAU. What respect? What are you talking about?

PARMIGIAN. The emperor of disease does not share a room with a nose job and a bunch of kidney stones!

LANDAU. I didn't realize there was such a hierarchy of disease.

PARMIGIAN. There's a hierarchy with everything in this world. You start off with an ameba and you end up with a tuna fish.

LANDAU. What about a whale?

PARMIGIAN. What about a whale?

LANDAU. Well, a whale's bigger than a tuna fish.

If you're going to create hierarchies for yourself, why not end up with a whale?

PARMIGIAN. Because a whale's a jerk compared to a tuna fish!

LANDAU. And what about human beings? Or don't they count?

PARMIGIAN. I'll tell you about human beings. A human being is an even bigger jerk than a whale. In my book the tuna fish is number one! It never gets cancer and it makes a terrific salad!

LANDAU. Well, if that's going to be the measure of everything for you, you ought to consider the cockroach. That never comes down with cancer, either!

PARMIGIAN. Then that's what's on top of the world: the cockroach and the tuna fish! (LANDAU *crosses Downstage Right.*) What's the matter? You think I'm trying to make a joke? You think I'm trying to amuse you? I have no time for stupidity! One million years from today when the last cancer cell has wiped out the last human being, and they visit us from outer space, you know what they're going to see? A cockroach and a tuna fish riding the BMT subway down to Wall Street!

LANDAU. (*Crosses to chair Stage Left of Stage Right table, sits down.*) And this is what you spend your entire thought process on? The circles of the world bounded by a cancer cell; the horizon no bigger than the back of a cockroach?

PARMIGIAN. Why do you make yourself such an absurd person, Landau? Do you think I would spend my entire thought process on a question an imbecile could answer for himself in two seconds? No, my friend, my dear Richard Landau, I am devoting my entire thought process to one question, and one question alone: What am I waiting for? What is it I am

waiting for? I am like a man in a dark passageway,
a man who has heard a door open somewhere, and
now waits to see what is coming . . . something silent
coming.

LANDAU. Maybe it's the rest of the ants coming to
pick up the rum cake you dropped all over the floor.

PARMIGIAN. Five thousand years of cabalistic training and that's the answer you give me? A bunch of
ants coming to pick up a piece of rum cake?

LANDAU. (*Suddenly, surprisingly angered.*) I don't
have any answers to give you! (*Rises.*) I don't have
any answers to give anyone! Five thousand years of
cabalistic training? Well, I haven't had any cabalistic
training! Not five thousand years! Not two thousand
years! Nothing! (*Grab wheelchair.*) You understand
that? Nothing! I am not a college graduate! I am not
a high school graduate! I didn't even have a chance
to . . . (LANDAU, *realizing that he has momentarily
lost control of himself, comes to an abrupt halt.*)

PARMIGIAN. To what?

LANDAU. (*Crosses Downstage Right.*) Nothing that
concerns you. I don't know why you keep bringing
this up. For a man who sees no point to the universe,
you have a pretty strange interest in mysticism.

PARMIGIAN. Jewish mysticism.

LANDAU. All right, Jewish mysticism.

PARMIGIAN. I keep bringing this up because you're
a Jew, and every Jew has an understanding of mysticism.

LANDAU. From what? Where am I supposed to get
this understanding? I'm not a scholar. I'm not a rabbi.

PARMIGIAN. From the bones. It comes from the
bones.

LANDAU. (*Crosses Left to* PARMIGIAN.) Nothing
comes from the bones! How can you have read every-

thing you say you've read, how can you talk about Hegel and Schopenhauer, and having found the secret of the universe, and still believe in such garbage? Bones? (*Crosses above* PARMIGIAN *to Stage Left of* PARMIGIAN, *continue to Downstage of bench.*) It's inbred in the bones? Well, let me tell you something. I've heard that kind of garbage before!

PARMIGIAN. Where was that?

LANDAU. Wherever you'd like it to be. Spain. France. Germany. In the back of a restaurant in Madrid. Wherever.

PARMIGIAN. (*Crosses Left to Left Center.*) What were you doing in back of a restaurant in Madrid?

LANDAU. (*Crosses Left,* PARMIGIAN *follows.*) I don't know why I said that. It doesn't mean anything to me.

PARMIGIAN. You were in all those places?

LANDAU. No place. I was no place.

PARMIGIAN. What were you doing in all those places? (*There is a certain manner in* PARMIGIAN's *speech and expression that brings* LANDAU *to a halt. For some moments he stares at* PARMIGIAN.)

LANDAU. You're not interested in mysticism at all.

PARMIGIAN. Tell me about all those places, Landau.

LANDAU. It's just something to talk about, just something else to talk about, isn't it?

PARMIGIAN. Tell me about Madrid, Landau. Tell me about the restaurant in Madrid.

LANDAU. Tell you about anything that isn't silence is what you mean! My life to fill your silence! You're interested in anything that isn't silence! It doesn't matter what it is, does it, Mr. Parmigian? It's all the same to you: the cabala, ants, re-runs on the television, anything, everything, as long as it isn't silence. (*Crosses Right above* PARMIGIAN *to Stage Right table, gets attache, gathers things at table.*)

PARMIGIAN. (*Crosses Right to Downstage of Center pole, level with* LANDAU.) Where are you going?

LANDAU. I'm going inside.

PARMIGIAN. What for? There's nothing inside.

LANDAU. There's nothing outside either, Mr. Parmigian.

PARMIGIAN. (*As* LANDAU *starts to exit.*) Landau! Don't leave me out here. Stay with me a little while. You don't have to talk. You don't have to say anything to me. Please. I don't want to be alone. I . . . I can't be alone no more.

LANDAU. Then go inside. You've got a whole floor full of people to feed yourself on.

PARMIGIAN. Who? The woman who sits in the dayroom, shuffling her cards? The rest of them who lie in their rooms, staring at the ceiling, dying with the spit running out of their mouths and a thousand tubes in their body? Who, Landau? Who?

LANDAU. (*Crosses Left to urn, put catalogue in attache.*) I don't know.

PARMIGIAN. Stay with me, Landau, for a little while, for a little while and then I won't bother you no more. Please, I can't be alone no more. (*As* LANDAU *turns from urn to cross Right.* LANDAU *slowly sits down again.*) I know what I am, but I also know what dying is. I'm being left alone here. I'm watching a world filled with things, with people, with a million adventures, slowly shutting me out, putting me aside, separating me from themselves. A little less attention every day, a little longer to answer the bell when you ring it. And the mind's not stupid. It sees what's happening . . . it sees . . . But it thinks it's going to go on living forever, no matter what the body tells it, no matter what it hears the doctors tell it—the truth is a lie it won't believe. You'd tell it yourself,

but you don't have the heart. And when death comes
—what? It must be a big surprise. The mind must be
stunned with surprise. It was just on the point of
making new worlds for itself, just on the point of telling me this roof garden is a Bounty from which I
will never mutiny, a Garden of Eden from which I
will never be thrown out. Give it the whole universe
and it wouldn't have enough room, or put it in a
little box and watch it make worlds within worlds,
little worlds without end. How such a thing could die,
I don't know. (*For a moment there is silence between
the* TWO MEN *as* PARMIGIAN *stares blankly forward,
and* LANDAU *is lost in his own thoughts.*) What do
you think about, Landau? When I ask you what you
are thinking of and you tell me you are thinking of
something else, or nothing?

LANDAU. Nothing.

PARMIGIAN. What does nothing look like?

LANDAU. Things . . . different things . . . a room
. . . (*Backward Upstage Left to drain.*) if there was
sunlight in the room . . . a dresser . . . a chair . . .
A man I once met in a police station in Portugal . . .
a man who wanted me to remember his name, and I
can't anymore. I don't think I was eight years old.

PARMIGIAN. What were you doing in a police
station?

LANDAU. My father was there somewhere. The war
had broken out that day . . . or some other day . . .
and we went around . . . I think it was just the two
of us because I don't remember my mother or sister
going with us into any of those buildings . . . embassies . . . maybe they were embassies because the
floors were marble . . . white marble . . . rosy marble
. . . so we had the day together, my father and I . . .
I didn't do that too often with him . . . it was nice

being alone with him . . . I must have liked that . . . I must have. (*Pause. Turn Right, Backward Right to* PARMIGIAN.) I'm sorry. What was your question?

PARMIGIAN. I asked you what you were doing in a police station in Portugal.

LANDAU. They were deporting some of the German Jews; I know that now because I read a lot about it, and I've written a lot of letters about it. You see, I have a file. In my dresser at home I kept a file about that. (*Pause.*) That man in the police station kept talking and talking.

PARMIGIAN. About what? (LANDAU *just looks blankly at him.*) About what, Landau?

LANDAU. I had some candy. My father had given me some candy and the man was hungry and he wanted it. He kept offering me things . . . things he had in his pockets. I finally gave him the candy for some money, or something else, something else that wasn't money!

PARMIGIAN. He must have made a strong impression on you to remember him so many years.

LANDAU. He was nothing to me! Just another Jew waiting to be sent away like the rest of them! (*Crosses Upstage to chair Stage Left of Stage Right table, sits.*) They (*Takes chair Stage Left to Right Center on level with* PARMIGIAN.) had him handcuffed to a chair, and he kept telling me how stupid it was, how he could lift up the chair and just walk out of the building with it if he wanted to. He had escape plans, a thousand different escape plans, if only he wasn't handcuffed. I was alone with him, and I was so frightened. I couldn't leave the room because my father had told me to stay there. I wasn't even allowed to get out of my chair. And the man is screaming and pulling and pulling on the handcuff, and his wrist is bleeding, and it's an old handcuff, or they didn't close it properly, and it opens up, and he is free. Free to escape. For one awful moment in his life, free of them. And he rubs his wrist, and sitting very quietly now in the chair, snaps the handcuff shut again.

PARMIGIAN. I don't understand.

LANDAU. Can't you? Can't you understand how a man could be more afraid of making a futile attempt to escape than of anything they could do to him if he tried? Well, it doesn't matter. (*Rises, crosses Right to rail edge and Downstage to Upstage Left of Stage Right table.*)

PARMIGIAN. Why do you always say that? "This doesn't matter. That doesn't matter." It's important that people understand each other.

LANDAU. They understand each other. It just never makes any difference.

PARMIGIAN. So tell me, and we'll see if it makes a difference.

LANDAU. (*Studying him for a moment before answering.*) He didn't want to be humiliated again, not laughed at again, not made a joke of again. Can you understand that? Really understand that? How a man could say to himself, "Better to take one final train ride to Hell, than live another day in Europe; better to let it end than have to listen one more time to Europe's murderers coming down a thousand dirty Jewish alleys?"

PARMIGIAN. I can understand that.

LANDAU. No . . . no . . . I will not let you say that . . . you cannot say that. No.

PARMIGIAN. Where are your parents that don't come to the hospital, Landau? Your sister?

LANDAU. They walked down an alley and they went away. I kept trying to run after them, but the stones were wet or slippery, and I couldn't keep my balance, and they were around the corner and they were gone— (*Crosses Downstage to Stage Right of* PARMIGIAN.) it was like the dog. My father had a dog and the dog got too big to be kept in the city, so we left him with a farmer, and the dog ran after the car, down the road, trying to catch up to us . . . trying, trying so hard not to be left behind—but they were gone; gone, like all the rest of them, the man in the police station—all gone away. I did a lot of research about this . . . about what they were doing with the German nationals they deported, and I have a file! In my dresser . . . I keep a file . . . about that. (*Take chair Stage Left, sits Stage Right of* PARMIGIAN, *talk intimately to him.*) You know I've been doing something very interesting since April. There was some Chinese cloisonne work on auction in this apartment on Park Avenue, this old apartment, but I wasn't there more than a few seconds before I realized that this apartment had the exact same layout as the apartment my parents rented in Munich. I had a difficult time keeping track of the auction. There were a lot of bids I wanted to enter, but it seemed to get so warm in the living room, and there was a hall, and I wanted to go down the hall. I felt embarrassed getting up, I was representing clients and there's a certain responsibility, but I went down the hall and stood by the kitchen and it was as if I could remember my mother doing the dishes in the kitchen, and my father in the dining room, sitting at the table with his books, studying, wearing that great heavy sweater of his—I always thought one day I'd have that sweater—and I knew down at the end of the hall there was a bathroom, because sometimes late at night I'd get out of bed to go to the hall bathroom, and I'd see the light still burning in the dining room, or he'd hear me as I passed by and call me in to sit with him by the table. I can't tell you what a feeling came over me standing there in this woman's apartment. My hands were trembling, I couldn't stop them, and inside me there was such a sense of overwhelming joy, my whole body felt alive again because this was something new, I had remembered something that wasn't there before, something that was lost . . . a table filled with medical books . . . I could . . . I could see the pictures . . . my father was in medical school then because they were medical books he was studying! When we lived in Munich my father was in medical school! And I walked over to the table and I could see him sitting there . . . months later . . . years later . . . maybe another apartment . . . his hands covered by a cloth because somebody had broken his hands . . . somebody . . . Did the Nazis break his hands? Did they break his hands under a brewer's cart? But the bedroom was wrong. It wasn't where my bedroom was, so . . . so what I've been doing that's very interesting since April is that I've been trying to figure out where my bedroom was.

PARMIGIAN. Why didn't they send you back, Landau? Why your family and not you?

LANDAU. My father found a man . . . Luis Boscan. And for money . . . I guess everything my father had left . . . he took care of me. His wife used to tell me that they would have taken my sister, too, but my mother was afraid to let her go . . . she was just a baby . . . it was a choice . . . It wasn't a matter of money . . . my mother made a choice. I . . . um . . . Anyway, they were nice people. I still write to them. Sometimes they write to me. They like to tell me about the time they met my father . . . where it was, what the day was like, what he was wearing . . . they always seem to find something new, some little detail . . . I . . . (*Standing up and walking away.*) I don't like talking about the Boscans. My life is a history of the Boscans! Their sons, and the businesses their sons went into! Their daughters and who they married! Their grandchildren! My life has a history that has nothing to do with the Boscans! It had a beginning! It had people in it! It had . . . It had . . . what did it have? What? I would sit by a window thinking the day would come when my father would walk around the corner of that alley again . . . my mother, my sister . . . my sister . . . Oh God. How many years did I sit by that window wishing they had saved her instead of me. Waiting! Waiting! Just like the rest of them. Waiting for passports that never arrived, waiting for boats that would take us out of there, waiting at the embassies, the British, the American, waiting to reach invisible people, diplomats who could save anyone, if only you could touch them—but you couldn't, because they hid themselves down corridors no refugee could enter, behind doors no Jew could open! A world died trying to touch these faceless people who had no pity, while I sat by a window— waiting!

PARMIGIAN. And later?

LANDAU. And later there was no later! Not for them. Not for me.

PARMIGIAN. No, Landau, that's not true. For you there was a later, and later you felt happy you were alive.

LANDAU. Is that what you think?

PARMIGIAN. I would have felt that way.

LANDAU. Yes. You would have. Anything to stay alive. In talking to you I am very aware of that. (*Rises, crosses Downstage Left.*)

PARMIGIAN. And what's wrong in wanting to stay alive?

LANDAU. Nothing. For you, nothing.

PARMIGIAN. And for you? What's wrong in wanting to stay alive, for you?

LANDAU. (*Crosses Left to urn.*) I don't want to talk about this.

PARMIGIAN. (*Crosses Left toward* LANDAU.) Why not? Because your parents threw you clear of a whirlpool that was sucking them down, and you don't know why you're happy you're alive?

LANDAU. No! Because being happy I'm alive doesn't mean anything to me! (*Crosses Right to* PARMIGIAN.) How can you be happy you're alive when you don't know who you are? When you have no yesterday, no past? When the only ground you have to stand on is the memory of what you were, and it's not there anymore? He's killed everything, cut off every link to what I was, so that even when I do remember I can never be sure it's true. He's killed, and He's killed, and I have no way back.

PARMIGIAN. Who's He, Landau?

LANDAU. You know Him. You sit in your chair waiting, and you know Him. You die in a concentration camp and His hand reaches into your mouth for the gold teeth and you know Him. A handcuff falls off your wrist and you think you can escape until His fingers snap it shut again, and you know Him. (*Crosses Right above* PARMIGIAN *to Right Center.*)

PARMIGIAN. There is no Him, Landau, just us.

LANDAU. How glib you are. I listened to you all afternoon going on and on as if you knew something that was worth all those words, and all I could think about was how every sound I make is unpleasant to me, how much I've grown to hate the sound of my own voice. I'm tired of being a man. Tired of putting on my clothes in the morning. Tired of taking them off at night. Tired of turning on the gas to broil a piece of meat and standing there with the match in my hand, watching it burn down till it scorches my fingers, forgetting what it was I came there to do. (*Looking directly at* PARMIGIAN.) And nothing of this has anything to do with you.

PARMIGIAN. That's absolutely true. That's why you should talk to me. I can give you a hundred percent objective opinion. That's what every Jew needs. A one hundred percent objective opinion from Armenia.

LANDAU. I don't need any opinions from you or anyone else.

PARMIGIAN. Excuse me, Landau. In my opinion I never met anyone who needed more opinions than you do. You remind me of a man with a club foot who tells everybody he's got a ballet slipper on his foot. Which reminds me of something in my dream with the King of Bavaria and his wife. In the dream for some strange reason I have turned myself into a hunchback. I walk around with a big hump on my back. What do you think about this?

LANDAU. Nothing!

PARMIGIAN. Another "nothing" from the master of "nothing." What's the matter, Landau, don't you see the similarity between our two cases? You with your club foot and me with my hump?

LANDAU. What similarity? There's no similarity! You just invented that! You just gave yourself a hump on the back when you decided to give me a club foot! You never dreamed you were a humpback until you decided I had a club foot! (LANDAU *turns away from him.*)

PARMIGIAN. Landau, you came out a winner.

LANDAU. Why? Because I survived?

PARMIGIAN. You not only survived, Landau, you triumphed! A boy with no education turns himself into a man who can almost tell the difference between a Van der Heyden, whatever that is, and a Pieter Bruegel. A boy dropped down in the middle of Portugal alone ends up in America with a wife, two children, and a ten speed bike. This is a triumph, Landau.

LANDAU. It doesn't feel like a triumph.

PARMIGIAN. That's because nothing we ever do feels like a triumph, because the mind's a piece of garbage. It's never happy with what we do for it. I once took my mind down to Barbados for two weeks, and you know what it said to me? "You should have taken us to Jamaica!" So don't wait around for thanks from it. I'll let you in on a little secret. The real reason Adam and Eve got thrown out of the Garden of Eden had nothing to do with a piece of fruit, because there's nothing wrong with a piece of fruit, it's a good laxative. What it was was that God finally got tired waiting around for thanks from the human brain. He said, "If I have to wait around for thanks, I'm going to die of old age. So screw it, and while I'm thinking about it, screw them!"

LANDAU. I thought you didn't believe in God.

PARMIGIAN. When did I say that?

LANDAU. (*Crosses Left to* PARMIGIAN.) A few minutes ago, right after you got done talking about pomegranates or plantains or whatever it was.

PARMIGIAN. Who remembers what I said a few minutes ago? Why do you live in the past? The past is a bunch of junk, too. Yesterday you were worried about the varicose veins in your wife's leg, today she bought herself a new bottle of perfume. Concentrate on the perfume. There's a new world coming in every twenty-two seconds.

LANDAU. You really believe that?

PARMIGIAN. Absolutely. Right now in a laboratory under the mountains of Zurich there's a man with one eye working on a new cure for cancer. It won't work, but that's what's happening in the present.

LANDAU. (*Crosses Upstage Left.*) Not my present, Mr. Parmigian.

PARMIGIAN. What is your present? A man tied to a chair in a Portuguese police station, talking to an eight year old boy?

LANDAU. (*Crosses Downstage to Stage Left of* PAR-MIGIAN.) That's right! That's my present! You think it helps anything listening to you reduce everything to an absurdity?

PARMIGIAN. And you? You think it helps anything listening to you reduce everything to a tragedy?

LANDAU. My God! What do you think it was? Don't you think it was a tragedy?

PARMIGIAN. No. It was worse than a tragedy. A tragedy doesn't even begin to get at it. It was a monument, Landau. A monument! Compared to what happened to you, Oedipus putting out his eyes was a minor occurrence.

LANDAU. And this is what I'm supposed to forget?

PARMIGIAN. You can't walk around with a monument, Landau. It's enough to walk around with a club foot.

LANDAU. (*Sits in Downstage Left chair.*) Leave me alone, Mr. Parmigian. I don't want to discuss this with you.

PARMIGIAN. Who do you want to discuss this with? A psychiatrist? You got a psychiatrist, Landau? Don't bother answering me. I can see from the way you twitch around in a chair you must have worn out a hundred leather couches already. (LANDAU *crosses Right to table.*) You know what you can do for fifty dollars an hour? You can visit five massage parlors and have a terrific time.

LANDAU. Stop it! Talking to you . . . trying to talk to you . . . and listening to this . . . it's . . . it's . . .

PARMIGIAN. Absurd? It's absurd, Landau?

LANDAU. It's humiliating! (*Face Upstage with head hung down.*)

PARMIGIAN. Of course, it's humiliating. You know why it's humiliating? Because no matter how many times you try to explain it to yourself, your wife, your psychiatrist, the man on the bus with the pince nez on his nose, it comes out a diminishment. Real suffering, Landau, real suffering is a catastrophe without language. It's a dinosaur egg big as a moon which cracks open with a two inch chicken inside of it. Don't you think I know this?

LANDAU. (*Sits in Stage Right chair.*) I don't know what you know. You turn everything into an absurdity.

PARMIGIAN. Only suffering. Only suffering. Look around you. Don't you notice something peculiar? Here is a terrific roof garden for the patients, but where are the patients? Why don't the patients use this terrific roof garden? You want an answer? They don't use this terrific roof garden because they know I'm out here. Inside is a dayroom with a woman sitting alone in it. Nobody will go in. They will walk by it because they know she's in it. When we're forced into the same room to watch a television show, you know what the entrance looks like? A bunch of leopards meeting for the first time in the jungle: a little nod of the head, a little acknowledgement that somebody might be alive besides ourselves, and that's it. At night you can hear the silence in the separate rooms like a dozen crystal chandeliers waiting to explode.

LANDAU. Then why talk to me? If that's what happens around here, why talk to me?

PARMIGIAN. Because you're a little bit of a fooler, Landau. A little bit of a trickster. When I saw Miss Latin America wheel you out here, I thought it was a hundred and seventy pounds of fresh meat arriving. There was a big skirmish in the hall for you, a collision of crutches and glucose bottles. They should have known you've been in the refrigerator for thirty-five years. That's why you don't care what happens to you with your exploratory, that's why you can sit out here and everything I say to you, "It's nothing." "It's not important." "It doesn't matter." I got a dazzling truth for you. You never got out of that police station alive! You're not waiting for a death sentence here, because you're still waiting for a death sentence from the time you were eight years old! Well, it's not going to happen! The judge is never coming back into the room, the jury fell asleep in the jury box, the executioner died with his victims, so as far as anybody cares you can get up and walk out!

LANDAU. (*Turn Left.*) How do you walk out of what's in your mind? How do you get up and walk out of what's in your mind?

PARMIGIAN. (*After working* LANDAU *up to a fevered pitch, the accusatory tone suddenly drops completely out of* PARMIGIAN's *voice.*) Who knows? I'm not a psychiatrist. This analysis is from a movie I once saw with Ingrid Bergman and Gregory Peck. Now in this movie . . . she got him all worked up to a big climax with an orchestra in the background, and there was a tremendous breakthrough. You got a breakthrough like that, Landau? (*They stare at each other for a few moments, and then* LANDAU *begins to laugh, a strange laugh that twists his mouth into a wry self-deprecating kind of contortion. He covers his mouth with his hands as if trying to hide the sound.*) You laughing? Is that what your laughing sounds like?

LANDAU. (*Lowering his hands.*) Oh, God.

PARMIGIAN. It's a joke, huh? A joke?

LANDAU. A very sad joke . . . pain into absurdity, memory into counterfeit.

PARMIGIAN. That's the thing. In this universe that's the only thing we got for a joke. With an orchestra, without an orchestra, it's still a watermelon with four legs. What we want from it is not coming. (*Looking down at the floor.*) What's coming here is an ant after a piece of rum cake.

LANDAU. (*Suddenly standing.*) His name was Reischmann! The man in the police station his name was Reischmann!

PARMIGIAN. (*Crosses Right to Center.*) Good for you. You remembered his name. You saved him from oblivion.

LANDAU. He gave me a glass paperweight for the candy. A millefiore glass paperweight. It couldn't have been very good. We never learned to make good glass paperweights in Germany.

PARMIGIAN. And you saved it all the days of your childhood. Huh, Landau?

LANDAU. No. Somewhere along the line I lost it. Somewhere here, somewhere there. (*Sits in chair Stage Right of Stage Right table.*) I'd like to remember it all very clearly: every blow, every hurt in every eye, the humiliation my father must have known cleaning dishes in a hundred dirty little restaurants so we could survive—and all that's really there are bits and pieces: a piece of glass you keep for a while and then you lose it or you throw it away, the Passover table set with crystal and lace, the strands of my sister's hair when she was all dressed up and proud . . .

PARMIGIAN. When I think of bits and pieces I think of a 1933 Buick I once had with a hundred and six patches on every tire.

LANDAU. (*Still lost in his own thoughts, not really listening to* PARMIGIAN.) I do some photography work now. It's a nice hobby. Summers I take pictures of the kids on the beach . . . birthdays and anniversaries, holidays when my wife's family comes over for dinner . . . and the pictures fill pages, and the pages fill albums, and one album sits stacked on another . . .

PARMIGIAN. You know, it would amaze you what you could do with a good patch. The patches on this 1933 Buick were so good that when the tires disintegrated the patches kept rolling for another hundred and seventy two miles. They ran over a state trooper who was giving a speeding ticket to a nun that looked like a penguin. (LANDAU *begins to laugh, a strange bitter laugh, banging his forehead with his fist.*) That's it, my friend, laugh a little bit, and while you're laughing I'll wait a little bit longer with you. I'll give the man working with one eye in the Zurich laboratory another month.

LANDAU. It probably won't make any difference. The Swiss never save anything but themselves.

PARMIGIAN. Even their cheese is full of holes.

LANDAU. He's probably an incompetent, the man in the laboratory.

PARMIGIAN. Absolutely. Worse than incompetent. How else do you think he lost his eye? (*For some moments,* BOTH MEN *laugh, sharing their private joke, and then* LANDAU *wipes his eyes, and reaches for his attache case.*)

LANDAU. (*Rises, crosses Upstage Center with briefcase.*) I'm going inside now, Mr. Parmigian. (*Walks toward the exit.*)

PARMIGIAN. Will you take me inside with you?

LANDAU. (*Turning and looking at* PARMIGIAN'S *upturned face for a moment.*) Yes. (*Crosses Downstage to Stage Right of* PARMIGIAN. *As* LANDAU *touches the back of* PARMIGIAN'S *wheelchair,* PARMIGIAN *reaches down and releases the brake.*)

PARMIGIAN. Look, off with the brake, off with everything, and I'm ready to roll. (*Pause.*) Landau?

LANDAU. Yes?

PARMIGIAN. I'll meet you out here tomorrow?

LANDAU. All right.

PARMIGIAN. Landau?

LANDAU. Yes?

PARMIGIAN. I promise you a very interesting day. (*Lights dim and out as they exit.*)

THE END

PROPERTY LIST

ACT ONE

Off Right—

(On escape platform) Parmigian wheelchair
(locked) with water bottle (filled), double straw,
blanket, cushion, tooth taped to left arm.

Prop Table:

Ice Iceam Sandwich (Madurga)

Parmigian eye glasses, rum cake in napkin, and
newspaper (Act Two)

Landau's eye glasses

On Stage—

s. r.: Table and 2 chairs with arms on u. s. marks

2 magazines on table (Esquire, Newsweek)

Brown attache case with catalogues, gold pen,
pad inside (closed) on s. c. chair

Landau wheelchair (locked) with Baby Ruth

s. l.:

Bench with flower box

u. s. l.:

Table and one (1) chair s. r. of table

Nail polish and remover, "Bride" magazine on
table

Personal Props—

Eye glasses, watch, wedding band (Landau)

Wallet with credit and membership cards (8)—
(Parmigian)

Engagement ring, watch (Madurga)

71

ACT TWO

Take attache case and glasses from Landau as he
exits

Strike:
Baby Ruth
All magazines
Nail polish and remover
Tooth
Landau wheechair

Set:
s. R. table and 2 chairs to Act Two positions
Parmigian wheelchair s. c. with blanket, refilled
water bottle
Brown attache case with blue and yellow papers
to U. C. railing with R. catch only fastened
Catalogues, pen, pad, eye glasses, eye glass case
on s. R. table (See diagram)
Stainless teapot with colored water, sugarbowl,
cup and saucer and spoon on U. L. table

Note: Get eye glasses and case and wallet with cards
from Parmigian
1 Wallet
2 Glasses
Rum cake